Goal Setting for Sport:

A Concise Guide for
Coaches and Athletes

Kevin Sivils

A Southern Family Publishing

KCS Basketball Enterprises, LLC
Katy, Texas

Goal Setting for Sport:
A Concise Guide for Coaches and Athletes

Copyright 2011 Kevin Sivils
All Rights Reserved
ISBN: 1461077931
ISBN-13: 978-1461077930

Cover Photography by David Shutts of Shutts Photography

Cover Design: Patricia Jonesi

Published by *A Southern Family Publishing*

A Division of KCS Basketball Enterprises, LLC

www.kcsbasketball.com

Dedication

This book is dedicated to all the athletes I have coached. Without our players, coaches have no real purpose nor can we achieve our goals. It is my hope this book helps other athletes, and coaches, achieve their dreams and goals.

Other Books by Kevin Sivils:

Game Strategy and Tactics for Basketball:
Bench Coaching for Success

The Game of Basketball:
Basketball Fundamentals, Intangibles and
Finer Points of the Game for Coaches, Players
and Fans

Integrating the Three-Point Shot Into
Your Offense

Delay Games – Holding the Ball:
Ten Different Delay Games

Finding Good Help:
Developing and Utilizing Student
Assistant Coaches

Secondary Break Offense:
Maximizing the Running Game

Offensive Building Blocks for Basketball

Contents

Introduction

Athletes and coaches alike have dreams, ambitions and goals. All too often nothing comes of these creative ideas because the athlete, or coach, never establishes a realistic plan to turn these dreams and goals into reality.

Goal setting is just the tool to make dreams become reality. The process is not a difficult one but it does require considerably more effort than simply stating a goal has been set.

A goal by itself cannot accomplish anything. A goal used properly and acted upon with passion can serve as a motivational tool, a source of feedback on performance, a measuring stick for progress and a means of evaluation after the goal has been achieved or abandoned.

Much of the goal setting process seems like common sense, and indeed, much of goal setting is common sense. Unfortunately, the average individual never stops to think about goal setting in a common sense fashion.

The purpose of this book, *Goal Setting for Sport: A Concise Guide for Coaches and Athletes*, is to help athletic minded individuals engage successfully in the goal setting process, allowing for greater success in all of their athletic endeavors. Goal setting, like many behaviors learned in competitive athletics, is of use in all aspects of human activity. The ideas and skills presented in this short book are transferable by the reader to an endeavor the reader engages in.

For the reader who is not a basketball coach or player, please understand basketball is the sport I have spent most of my life playing and coaching. While I hope this book finds its way into the hands of athletes and coaches of many different sports, please bear with my use of basketball in the majority of the examples in the text of this book.

Chapter One

Goal Setting – Making Dreams Reality

One of my favorite stories about children and sports involves a little boy playing baseball alone in the family yard. The boy talks out loud to himself, setting the stage. It is game seven of the World Series, bases are loaded with two outs and the little boy represents the go-ahead run.

He tosses the ball into the air and swings with all his might. The bat misses the ball and the little boy shouts, "strike one!" He picks up the ball and tosses it into the air again. The ball is too far for him to take a swing and he confidently declares the pitch a "ball!" The process continues until the batter reaches a full count.

The boy now plays the role of both batter and radio announcer and sets the stage for the pay-off pitch. As little boys are so fond of doing, he plays out the famous story of the Great Bambino, the Sultan of Swat, more commonly known as Babe Ruth, "calling his shot" by pointing where he is going to hit the game winning home run

With the pressure of the entire series weighing down on the young batter's shoulders, he tosses the ball into the air for the pay-off pitch. He swings and....misses, striking out to end the game.

The boy looks around to see if anyone is paying attention and then leaps triumphantly in the air and once again plays the role of the radio announcer, shouting wildly, "what a pitcher, what a pitcher!"

Sports fantasies such as this are commonplace and part of the fun of sports. It also explains adult fantasy sports leagues where adults can live out the fantasy of being the owner, GM and coach of their own team.

When I practiced free throws as a basketball player, I always imagined different scenarios to make the repetitive task of free throw shooting more interesting. I won many a championship game at the foul line with no time remaining! It was all in my mind of course, but it certainly made practice more fun.

For some individuals these dreams become more than just a dream, they become reality. Players desiring to make their dreams of being a starter, playing their sport in college, the Olympics or turning pro, use goal setting to make the dream come true. The same is true for championship teams.

Unlike many skills taught to athletes by coaches of all sports, goal setting is a skill that will have direct and applicable lifelong use for every player, regardless of their vocation, hobbies or life ambitions. Turning dreams into reality takes work.

Setting goals is a tool to be used in the process of making those dreams come true.

Chapter Two

Types of Goals

What is a goal? Are there different types of goals? Does the type of goal set matter in helping the individual achieve the desired outcome? The answers to these questions are important and relevant to the individual or team achieving the desired outcome.

Defined simply, a goal is attaining a specific, defined level of skill or proficiency in a task or a desired specific outcome, usually within a specified amount of time. This definition provides a good general understanding of what a goal is, but it is hardly all encompassing in defining types of goals, the purpose of different types of goals and how these different types of goals aid in the process of achieving the desired outcome.

McClements (1982) further differentiated types of goals by defining subjective goals, general objective goals and specific objective goals. Examples of subjective goals would include making friends by being on a team, having fun playing a sport or learning how to be a good teammate.

General objective goals would include winning a tournament or a team championship or earning a roster spot on the varsity. Specific objective goals are further refined and begin to define specific objectives. Examples would include improving free throw percentage, batting average or yards per carry.

Goals can be further defined as outcome goals and performance goals. Outcome goals are specific in nature to a single, defined outcome such as winning a specific game, tournament or championship. Performance goals are specific in nature as well but geared to specific performance behaviors such as improving individual and team performance against specific standards of excellence or improving on past performances such as a specific score for a gymnast, time for the mile run or team free throw percentage.

What type of goals are the most effective. Research indicates the type of goal plays a major role in motivation. Botterill (1977) found group goals to be more effective and difficult goals were more effective in improving or enhancing performance than easy goals. It was also found that explicit goals were more effective than broad general goals, the best combination of goals were difficult, specific group goals.

Chapter Three

How Do Goals Influence Athletes?

Goals, if used correctly by athletes, are valuable tools in effectively shaping athlete's skills, focus, attitude and a multitude of other behaviors critical to success in athletic competition. Goals help to shape athletes in four key areas: directing the athlete's attention, focus and action to the most important elements of the task or skill, aiding the player in generating needed effort, extending or increasing persistence in performing a task and aiding athletes ability to focus on key mental strategies and tactics. Goals also provide athletes with a necessary sense of control and means of evaluation.

Goals directly influence an athlete's behavior by bringing a clear focus and attention to the details of performing essential components of skills necessary for success. For example, a basketball player who struggles at the foul line has, with the help of the coach, identified the key flaw in shooting technique. In this example the flaw is shooting the ball with too little arc, producing a flat trajectory. Correcting this is a matter of holding a high follow through. The basketball player sets a goal of having a follow through with the elbow above the eyebrow for 95% of all free throw attempts in practice and games.

The goal set in this example brings sharp focus on the part of the basketball player on the critical flaw in technique that must be corrected for both the player and the team to have success.

Identifying and quantifying the amount of effort and work needed to successfully complete a task can be daunting when the sheer volume of effort required is determined. Carefully set goals can help an athlete overcome the disillusionment experienced when evaluating the effort required.

A runner who has decided to train for a marathon might not pursue this objective after looking at the typical training plan to prepare for a marathon. A systematic approach using goals to guide the runner through each phase of the training makes the task less daunting. Success breeds a desire for more success and achieving the intermediary goals in progression provides the runner with a tangible measure of success and accomplishment.

It is understandable when faced with a difficult task that offers little hope of ever easing in difficulty that an athlete might give up. The offensive lineman who must block the relentless All State pass rusher is more likely to give his best effort every down if he has goals that aid in his understanding of why he must succeed in his blocking efforts. If the lineman's team runs the spread offense and throws on a majority of downs, a high percentage of hurries, sacks or hits on the quarterback will dramatically lower the offensive efficiency of the lineman's team.

The coaching staff must clearly explain the negative impact of not protecting the quarterback adequately. This information should then be combined with goals for the lineman in terms of how many hurries, etc, are permissible and will still allow the offense to be productive. Performance goals measured in real, definable terms provide offensive lineman with a very specific motivator.

The task is no longer defined in the daunting terms of going head-to-head with a dominating opponent. Instead the task is defined in measurable terms, allowing immediate feedback each play on the success or failure of the lineman's blocking. To make the task even more encouraging to the lineman, the goals should be defined in positive instead of negative terms. Instead of limiting the great pass rusher to two sacks and five hurries, the goal of the lineman could include two pancakes or to block the pass rusher beyond the quarterback and out of the passing play 90% of the time.

Control might be the most important aspect of setting goals. So many variables are involved in athletics, regardless of the sport, that many athletes feel overwhelmed and powerless. Goals, when used appropriately and well defined, provide athletes with a sense of control, that the athlete can manage the many variables. Goals focus an athlete's attention on single tasks or strategies. Moving through these in a sequential order, one goal, task or strategy at a time provides athletes with a manageable checklist.

As the event progresses, the athlete works through the checklist. This provides the athletes with a sense of control by limiting the variables to be dealt with and at the same time provides a measurable sense of accomplishment as each item or variable is dealt with successfully.

Despite the best efforts and well-planned, appropriate goals, athletes will experience failure. Goals provide a means to measure performance and evaluate causes of success and failure. Athletes will persevere if they learn from mistakes. For many athletes, learning how to overcome past failures is a powerful motivator. The evaluation process helps athletes and coaches determine what went wrong and the best method of correcting the mistake in order to enable future success.

Chapter Four

Ten Guidelines for Goal Setting

1) Set challenging but realistic goals

Competitive people like challenges. An easy achievement is nice, even necessary once in awhile. A steady diet of easy, non-challenging tasks leads to boredom, complacency and for many athletes, a loss of interest in the sport.

Dreams usually involve winning the "big game." Goals help break the road to achieving the dream into manageable stages of a journey. A goal needs to be challenging to make achieving the goal worthwhile and interesting, in order to maintain an individual's interest.

Care must be taken to strike a balance between challenging and realistic goals. An unrealistic goal that cannot be obtained serves to discourage individuals and teams, raising the danger of introducing "learned helplessness." This often leads to despair and in some instances leads to loss of interest in the activity.

A wide receiver wants to lower his 40 time from 4.9 seconds to 4.3 seconds. Given the limits of genetics, this is certainly a challenging goal but it is also an unrealistic one. Regardless of how hard the wide receiver works or how committed he is to sticking to his speed improvement and conditioning program, lowering his 40 time a full six tenths of a second is not physically possible. As the wide receiver continues to strive to meet the goal and begins to realize achieving the goal is impossible, discouragement will set in and in most instances the player will abandon the conditioning program as a futile exercise, regardless of any improvement in speed if the unrealistic goal cannot be achieved.

Setting a goal to lower the time from 4.9 seconds to 4.7 seconds is still a challenge. It is a realistic goal if the wide receiver is committed to following the plan set to achieve that goal. As the player works through the program and sees slow, but steady improvement towards the desired goal, the level of commitment to achieve the goal will not only remain steady, it will likely increase the closer the wide receiver comes to reaching the desired goal.

The key for this first guideline to be successful in the goal setting process is for the goal to be challenging, which makes achieving the goal worthwhile, yet realistic, making the goal one the athlete knows is achievable through hard work and commitment.

2) Goals must be specific and focused

Effective goals are as specific and tightly focused as possible. Becoming the greatest volleyball team of all time is certainly a dream and it can certainly be a goal. As stated it is not a particularly effective goal as it lacks the specificity required to make the goal both effective and a source of motivation for the athletes making up the team. The goal as defined is too broad and lacks focus.

The goal becomes more effective when the specific tasks a great volleyball team must possess are included as individual goals for the players. The more specific each goal is, the greater the likelihood the players will be able to understand the need to reach each goal and what the benefit of achieving that goal is. Goals too broad in nature do not bring the focus needed to motivate the volleyball players.

Championship volleyball teams all share the common trait of having a great serving percentage. One volleyball team sets a goal of "having a great serving percentage." Another volleyball team sets a series of goals related to team serving percentage, including a goal of serving at a 98% success rate, another goal of 10% of all serving errors being due to foot fault, 80% due the serve being too long and the final goal being the other 10% of errors due to serves going out on either sideline.

The first volleyball team's goal of having a great serving percentage is of little help in improving play. The second team's goals are specific and focus not only the rate of desired success, but explicitly define how the errors are to be made. The second team's goals provide clarity of purpose each time a player makes a single individual serve for the duration of the season.

3) Goals must be measurable

Goals must be measurable. It seems like an obvious statement, but many goals are set with little to no thought of how the goal is to be measured and as a result the individual or team who set the goal has no way to determine if the goal was met or means to evaluate the goal.

Goals must be challenging to work effectively. Challenging goals require effort and often take time to achieve. With no visible means of measuring progress towards the desired goal, it is difficult for athletes to maintain the necessary motivation to continue to work to meet the goal. Seeing progress and improvement can be a powerful motivating factor to keep athletes working towards achieving their goals.

4) Effective goals are written

Effective goals are written in clear, concise language, leaving no doubt about the objective of the goal and how the goal is to be achieved. Every detail and step involved, what must be focused on to achieve the goal and a specific deadline must be included.

Creating a written goal makes the goal more tangible, real and measurable. It also allows for accountability and evaluation at a later date. A written goal makes it visual and physically tangible for the athlete or team who set the goal.

5) *Effective goals have a deadline*

Deadlines create a sense of urgency. It really is that simple. If a goal is open ended and has no clear end point, the goal does not provide the specificity required to act as a motivating factor in the process of working to achieve the goal.

Deadlines also make the goal real. Steps must be taken now in order to achieve the goal by the deadline. As each of the intermediate steps is completed, the athlete can see progress towards the achievement of the desired goal.

6) *Effective goals are flexible*

Not all goals can be achieved. Some goals are poorly defined, the deadline is too soon, the goal is not easily measured or no intermediate goals have been set to reach the ultimate goal. This is does not mean the ultimate goal must be abandoned.

Instead goals must be flexible, allowing the athlete to modify the goal and still feel the goal has meaning. Extending a deadline is acknowledgement of the fact the first deadline was not realistic, nothing more.

Flexibility in goal setting allows athletes to change and modify goals as necessary rather than abandoning the final goal. This allows goals to continue to serve as a source of motivation and direction rather than becoming a source of discouragement.

7) *Effective goal setting utilizes a series of smaller, sequential goals progressing towards the ultimate goal*

Big goals, the kind that fulfill dreams, are often far in the distance. The distance and effort required to achieve the goal can be so daunting the individual or team who set the goal soon become discouraged by the seeming lack of progress in achieving the goal or the sheer volume of effort and sacrifice requirednnn.

Small, progressive, sequential goals provide measurable progress. The effort and commitment required to achieve each goal is manageable. As each of the smaller, sequential goals is progressively accomplished, the individual is able to feel a sense of achievement and accomplishment while progressing towards the ultimate big dream goal at the same time. The achievement of the small, sequentially progressive goals maintains a high level of motivation and commitment to meeting additional goals as well as the ultimate goal.

8) *Effective goals are performance oriented*

An outcome goal, win a championship or win a specific tournament, is a win or lose proposition. An outcome goal focuses on nothing more than the outcome.

Performance goals are much more effective in helping the individual or team to achieve the same desired outcome. Performance goals focus the attention on the controllable factors that will lead to success. Examples for basketball include free throw shooting percentage, defensive field goal percentage, rebound margin, etc. All of these factors are keys to winning a basketball game. Achieving the standards of performance goals such as these will likely lead to victory in the game.

There is nothing wrong with setting an outcome goal. Outcome goals are often strong motivating goals. The key to successfully achieving an outcome goal is the combined use of smaller, sequential goals and performance goals.

9) Effective goals are determined by the individual or team and not an outsider

Goals set by another person often have little or no importance for the individual who is expected to achieve the goal. The reason for this is quite simple. The individual, or team, who is expected to achieve the goal had no voice in the creation of the goal resulting in a feeling powerlessness or lack of control.

Setting a goal is an act of control. It grants a sense of ownership to the individual or team who determined the goal. Control is essential for the goal to act as a motivator. Failure to have control over the goal setting process will result in a set of goals individual athletes and teams see no reason to struggle and sacrifice to achieve.

10) *Effective use of goals requires evaluation and follow-up*

Regardless of whether or not a goal is successful or a failure, evaluation and follow-up is essential for the success of future goals. Ineffective goals can provide valuable information for future goal setting and evaluation of performance.

Successful goals can be just as valuable in the evaluation process because these goals demonstrate what is effective and what works. Performance goals, when achieved, serve to reinforce effective strategies, tactics and execution of skills and aid the athlete or team in future performances. The achievement of goals and developing an understanding of why the goals were successfully achieved creates insight into what is required for a quality performance and has the added benefit of building confidence in future success.

Follow-up is essential after the evaluation process. It allows mistakes to be corrected and valuable lessons to be reinforced and utilized again in future performances.

Chapter Five

Ten Common Goal Getting Errors

1) Goals that are too easy

Effective goals are challenging but obtainable. It is the challenge that motivates and directs. Goals that are too easy to obtain neither challenge nor inspire, making the goal ineffective.

2) Too broad and general

Providing focus, clarity and direction are key reasons to set goals. Broad, general goals do not provide needed focus, clarity or direction in order to provide necessary motivation and guidance to achieve the desired outcome.

3) Setting unrealistic expectations or outcomes as goals

Unrealistic goals lead to frustration and failure. Not every athlete can become a professional athlete or play intercollegiate athletics. Every athlete and team can improve and be more successful. Goals must be challenging, but realistic.

4) Not directly applicable to the task

For a goal to be effective, it must be directly related to the task, skill or desired outcome. Setting the goal of becoming a master portrait painter is a worthy goal, but it will not improve free throw shooting or shave tenths of a second off a 100-meter sprint.

5) Developing an incoherent plan

A clearly defined set of goals designed with a progression of intermediate goals using a good mix of performance based goals complete with deadlines, flexibility and a means to evaluate as the plan is worked helps tremendously in achieving the desired outcome. An incoherent plan lacks direction as well as all the other necessary elements for an effective plan. The lack of clear direction spreads the athlete's, or team's, efforts in a variety of directions, preventing clear progress from being made.

6) Goals set by an outsider – not the participant

Nothing can kill the value of goals as quickly as a sense of lack of control on the part of the individual or team responsible for carrying out the tasks required to achieve the goals. It is essential the individuals or team have input in the creation of the goal or goals. It is their dreams that are to be fulfilled. This does not mean guidance is unnecessary. It does mean control over the goal setting process must be shared.

7) Inflexible goals

What happens when a team loses the first game in league play and the team goal was to post an undefeated record in league play? The very nature of the goal limits the chance for success due to the inflexible nature of the goal. What is the team to do after losing the first contest of league play? The failure of the goal at the start of league play has the potential for a collapse in interest for the rest of the season.

Setting a goal of winning the league title is still challenging but includes margin for error. The loss of the first game of league play could serve as a powerful motivating factor for the remainder of the season as the team works to achieve the still valid goal.

8) Outcome goals used when performance goals were more appropriate

It is entirely possible to have a great performance and still not prevail in an athletic competition. Contests in which both competitors had outstanding performances are rebroadcast repeatedly on television and now the internet. Yet, only one team won the competition. Does this lesson the brilliance of the performance of the two competitors? What about classic championship tennis matches?

By limiting goals to only achieving an outcome, a real danger exists of ultimately creating a spirit of disillusionment and a loss of focus. Using performance goals as a means of evaluation has the benefit of focusing performance on the specific factors that lead to victory.

Using the two types of goals allow teams and individuals to have success even if the desired outcome, victory in the contest, is not achieved. This approach allows both competitors to feel a sense of satisfaction in the aftermath of the outstanding competitive effort.

9) No written plan

Putting things in writing establishes clarity and makes the concepts listed real. Simply keeping the plan in one's head allows the individual to easily set aside the goals and plan of action when it becomes inconvenient. Written goals also make it less likely the goals will be modified on a whim when the goals become too challenging or a distraction.

10) No method of evaluation or follow-up

All goals requiring significant effort, time and commitment and are worth achieving need to be evaluated and followed up once the plan has been completed. This step is essential to learn why the plan succeeded or failed, offering opportunities to learn for future endeavors. The information gained this way has great value and often serves as a power source of motivation in future endeavors.

Failure to provide either a mechanism to evaluate and follow-up a plan after its completion or the simple failure to attempt to engage in evaluation and follow-up will result in a loss of valuable information and insight.

Chapter Six

Goal Setting Procedures for Athletes

Achieving goals not only helps athletes win competitions, it is a significant factor in the improvement process of an athlete. Setting goals allows athletes to convert their dreams into reality.

Goal setting is not a magical process, nor a substitute for hard work, commitment and sacrifice. It is a valuable tool in the process of achieving success and improving, but only if used correctly by the athlete.

Converting the dream

Athletes are dreamers and the favorite dream of an athlete is achieving at the highest level of their sport and winning the championship. Making the dream a reality requires converting the dream into a plan based on goals.

Do your homework

Of the many reasons athletes never convert their dreams into reality is the simple fact the individual never confronts what is required to make the dream come to pass.

In order to establish goals, the athlete must have the requisite knowledge of what must come to pass in order to make the dream a reality. Some examples of factors to be considered include: how long will the training process take, what is the financial cost, what kind of coaching will be required, what equipment and facilities, if any, are necessary and what conflicting factors exist.

All of these questions plus countless others are possibly part of the equation in making the athletic dream a reality. Before a realistic goal setting program can be put in place, the athlete must do the necessary homework and research every possible factor to be dealt with.

Challenging but realistic

Boredom has a way of taking the fun out of sport. The best experiences in sport are competitive and challenging. Goals should be the same. Goals capable of being achieved with ease lead to enthusiasm killing boredom. Goals achieved with difficulty inspire to greater effort and a sense of fulfillment when achieved.

If challenging goals are better, should an athlete set the most difficult goals possible? The answer is maybe. Goals must be challenging while being realistic. Unrealistic goals lead to frustration so great the athlete will develop what sport psychologists call *learned helplessness*.

Simply defined, learned helplessness occurs when an athlete only experiences failure. The athlete learns to expect frustration and failure, a sense of helplessness. This will lead to a loss of passion and enthusiasm for the sport and the athlete will quit. Balance must be found between goals that challenge and goals that are realistic.

Divide the journey into manageable steps

When a runner makes the decision to enter their first marathon, the training regimen may seem so daunting the runner feels it is not possible to achieve their goal of completing the marathon.

The key to this is setting lots of intermediate goals. It is not necessary, nor advisable to run 20 miles in the fifth or sixth day of training. Instead the runner must set goals of ever increasing distance following a prescribed running plan. In time, the runner will achieve the larger goal of completing the 20-mile training run. The intermediate goals allow the runner to progress in training, stay motivated and to improve at a challenging but realistic rate.

Develop a timeline

When using intermediate goals to achieve a larger, more difficult goal, it is essential to develop a timeline. Setting deadlines provides a sense of urgency, a need to keep working to meet and achieve goals, to persevere when boredom or adversity occur.

Timelines, like goals, must be challenging but realistic. If the established deadlines become too difficult, athletes may simply readjust the timeline and make it more realistic.

Be flexible

The most carefully designed set of goals might not workout in the manner the athlete intended. Unforeseen or uncontrollable factors such as illness or injury could alter conditions rendering the planned goals unrealistic or unsuitable.

Instead of abandoning the larger, end goal, the athlete must take a flexible approach. No set of planned goals and the accompanying timeline is perfect when put in to practice. Flexibility and adaptability are the key guiding factors to be used when actually implementing a planned set of goals.

As the athlete works through the timeline and planned intermediate goals, there must be a willingness to be adaptable and flexible. Goals and timelines must be adjusted to meet the changing conditions and variables the athlete encounters. If goals prove to be too easy, make the goals more challenging. If goals prove to be too difficult, create more realistic and achievable goals.

Take ownership

Goals are not effective if set by another individual or group. The athlete, or team, must set their own goals for the goals to be meaningful and useful.

Coaches have a role in the goal setting process, but by and large, the athlete or team must set their own goals.

Plan the plan and then work the plan

Invest the time to complete all the necessary research, to establish performance goals, intermediate goals and outcome goals. Develop challenging but realistic goals and create a timeline with deadlines that are also challenging but realistic. Build in flexibility and be willing to adapt as necessary. Once the plan and timeline are established, stick to the plan and "work it!" Goals and a plan are of no value if the athlete, or team, do not utilize the plan!

Write the plan down

There is something about writing down goals, deadlines and ideas about adapting that make everything in the plan more tangible and real. Not only should the goals, accompanying timeline and other details of the plan be written down, the athlete or team must post the plan where it can be seen and viewed constantly. The written plan serves as a reminder of what is to be achieved!

Keep records

As the plan is being followed, notes should be taken about the level of difficulty of the goals, the challenges encountered, and as goals are met, checked off as successfully completed.

Record keeping is essential for goals to have maximum impact. Records allow for effective evaluation to be done in the future. Records allow for effective evaluation of past goals and creation of future goals.

Records allow the athlete or team to have a visual means of noting the completion of goals, to feel a sense of accomplishment and progress towards achieving the ultimate goal. Records allow the athlete or team to note improvement is taking place. Measured, continued improvement may be the greatest motivator there is.

Heed the wisdom of others to a point

Coaches and other experienced athletes can provide excellent and helpful feedback, even if critical, to a set of goals and the plan to implement the goals. This advice should be heeded, to a point. Balance the value of the constructive criticism and the experience of the coach or athlete providing the feedback against the dream.

If the critical feedback makes the plan more realistic and effective, use the feedback to modify the original plan.

When should the feedback of others who have experience, wisdom and a deep level of knowledge about the sport be ignored? Sadly, some individuals will not want an athlete or team to succeed and will provide feedback designed to kill the dream and prevent success.

Having said this, if the feedback is overly critical or "dream killing" in nature, seek another opinion. The individual who provided the feedback may very well be correct and providing appropriate feedback. Contrast the initial feedback with input from other individuals with experience and knowledge about the sport or activities in question. Be willing to seek advice about altering goals to achieve the desired outcome or level of performance. Always be flexible and realistic. It is your dream to achieve.

Evaluate when done

When the plan has been completed and the desired outcome achieved, or not, it is time to evaluate. Detailed records are of great value during this process. Examine the plan for what worked well, what did not and what could be improved upon. Take additional notes based on the evaluation and use all the information and experienced obtained from using the first set of goals in planning the next set of goals.

Chapter Seven

Goal Setting Procedures for Coaches

Goal setting is just as essential and valuable for coaches as it is for athletes and teams. The approach coaches must take is twofold in nature. The first is setting goals for the coach and this approach differs only slightly from the approach used by the players.

The second approach involves guiding athletes or a team in setting goals for themselves. This is quite different from setting goals for oneself and requires a different approach for the goal setting process to be effective for everyone involved.

Have a plan: Control what you can control

There are too many factors involved in a single season for a coach to attempt to control each variable. What can be done is to identify the variables that can be controlled, or at least influenced, and develop a plan to control these factors as best as possible. Let the rest go.

Divide the season

Successful coaches are generally good planners. They possess what might be described as a "warriors mentality." They identify every possible thing that could go wrong and prepare and rehearse a plan to deal with each eventuality.

To prepare an athlete or a team for each possible situation by the first competition of the season is not realistic. Being prepared by the start of league play or the play-offs is a realistic goal.

The first step in the planning process is to divide the season into manageable segments. These should include: the off-season, conditioning, pre-season, early season games, mid-season games, league play and play-offs.

Each segment of the season, or athletic year, must have its own plan and accompanying goals for both the coaching staff, the individual athletes and the team. Careful planning must be used in creating these goals as each stage of the athletic year builds to achieving the ultimate set for the entire season.

Let go

For goal setting to truly be effective, the coach has to let go. Their role in the goal setting process is to be a guiding force for the athletes and the team. Failure to allow the players to have significant input in the process will result in ineffective goal setting. This does not mean coaches do not have a big role in the process. The coaching staff must recognize the players need a sense of ownership of the goal setting process and the resulting goals that are established. A coach must let the players and team set goals that might not be quite in line with what the coaching staff wants.

Teach and guide

The true role of the coach in the goal setting process, and where a coach CAN exert considerable influence on the goals set, is teaching athletes and the team how to effectively set goals, monitor and evaluate goals and if need be, adjust goals as the season progresses. The time invested in teaching athletes and a team how to effectively set goals often results in excellent goals with only a little guidance to nudge the goals towards reality on the part of the coach.

Monitor record keeping

Record keeping is critical for the success of goals. Younger athletes and teams often resist record keeping as it can be tedious and time consuming. The coach must not only insist records be kept, but must monitor the process and aid the athletes and team in understanding the value of keeping records. This is a key component of the teaching and guiding role of the coach in the goal setting process.

Guide the evaluation process

The final step in the process of using goals is evaluating the effectiveness of the goals and the plan developed to achieve the desired goals. This is another role for the coach as teacher and guide. Athletes often will not take the time to self-examine appropriately and need to be taught how to do so. This includes evaluating goals and the effectiveness of the goal setting plan developed.

Chapter Eight

The Power of Goals: A Real Example

1988-89 - The LHSAA Top 24

Today this marquee event is known as the LHSAA Top 28. In 1988-89 it was the Top 24. In just the 4th season of the program's existence, the Runnels Raiders boy's basketball team won its first District 11-C championship and made a miraculous run through the state play-offs to reach the vaunted LHSAA Top 24 State Basketball Tournament. By the way, the season played out exactly as planned.

The spring before the players that would comprise the 1988-89 team sat down and engaged in the goal setting process. It was detailed and focused, the final objective on the list, a berth in the Top 24.

The members of that team never lost focus. They practiced hard and overcame adversity. The players did everything they had to achieve their goals, and in particular, the dream goal of reaching the Top 24. Luck you say? Perhaps some was involved. But I find good teams that are focused make their own luck. They find a way to win and this team certainly did that.

Just how powerful are goals when it comes to achieving dreams? I learned a valuable lesson that day in March of 1989.

The Raiders went down in defeat to eventual state champion Atlanta High School. They were better than us and they deserved to win. I had to attend the post-game press conference and upon entering the team dressing room I found my players in tears and in a mood to apologize. I was amazed by their reaction. They had achieved everything on their list of goals. It had been a magical season ending in a loss in the State Tournament! I told them they had nothing to be ashamed of. They had represented themselves, their team and their school in an outstanding fashion!

Then, with tears in his eyes, the captain of the team, Michael Peebles, explained the source of their discomfort by saying, "Coach, we set our goals too low. We were content to reach the semi-finals. We did not dig down deep enough to find a way to win like we have time and time again this season. It is all our fault." *I have to point out Atlanta defeated us by 30 points.*

Still, that moment in time remains etched in my mind like it just happened. Could we have beaten Atlanta? I do not know. But my players think they could have, if they had just set the right goals!

Realistically, Atlanta was just too good for us. We got as far as we could on our talent, hard work and the coaching I was able to provide as a young coach, and yes, we were a little lucky. But there is no doubt in my mind the importance the goals set by that group played in the achievements accomplished by that team. Without all the intermediary outcome goals, the performance goals, the difficult but challenging goals, the checklists and accountability sessions, the lofty goal of reaching the Top 24 would not have been met. The 1988-89 Runnels Raiders forever made me a believer in the value of goal setting when done correctly!

References

Botterill, C. (1977, September). *Goal setting and performance on an endurance task.* Paper and Sport Psychology Conference, Banff, Alberta, Canada.

McClements, J. (1982). Goal setting and planning for mental preparations. In L. Wankel & R.B. Wilberg (Eds.), Psychology of sport and motor behavior: Research and Practice. *Proceedings of the Annual Conference of the Canadian Society for Psychomotor Learning and Sport Psychology.* Edmonton, Alberta, Canada: University of Alberta.

About the Author

A 25 year veteran of the coaching profession, with twenty-two of those years spent as a varsity head coach, Coach Kevin Sivils amassed 464 wins and his teams earned berths in the state play-offs 19 out of 22 seasons with his teams advancing to the state semi-finals three times. An eight time Coach of the Year Award winner, Coach Sivils has traveled as far as the Central African Republic to conduct coaching clinics. Coach Sivils first coaching stint was as an assistant coach for his college alma mater, Greenville College, located in Greenville, Illinois.

Coach Sivils holds a BA with a major in physical education and a minor in social studies from Greenville College and a MS in Kinesiology with a specialization in Sport Psychology from Louisiana State University. He also holds a Sport Management certification from the United States Sports Academy.

In addition to being a basketball coach, Coach Sivils is a classroom instructor and has taught U.S. Government, U.S. History, the History of WW II, and Physical Education. He has served as an Athletic Director and Assistant Athletic Director and has also been involved in numerous professional athletic organizations.

Sivils is married to the former Lisa Green of Jackson, Michigan, and the happy couple are the proud parents of three children, Danny, Katie, and Emily. Rounding out the Sivils family are three dogs, Angel, Berkeley, and Al. A native of Louisiana, Coach Sivils currently resides in the Great State of Texas.

Team Orders

Team pricing is available for coaches who wish to order multiple copies of ***Goal Setting for Sport: A Concise Guide for Coaches and Athletes.*** For information on team orders please contact the author via e-mail at kcsbasketball@comcast.net.

Made in the USA
Coppell, TX
13 April 2021

53713251R00033